# ♥ ROMANCE 101 ♥

~~~

101 Creative & Fun Ideas
To Keep Your Marriage
Alive & Sparking

~~~

Ruth Claren

Romance 101 ... 101 Creative & Fun Ideas To Keep Your Marriage Alive & Sparking

ISBN 0-9686613-1-9

www.two-gether.com

♥ *Dedication* ♥

*To my
one and only
Simon Sinclair Clarence*

Ecclesiastes 4:9 & 12

♥ *Special Thanks To* ♥

My supporters/encouragers/editors/proofreaders:

Mr. Ken & Mrs. Doris Rome
Dr. Paul Rome
Mrs. Cheryl Chiesa
Rev. Rosswell Olson
Rev. William Olson
Dr. Gordon Franklin
Mrs. Robina Baker

~ ~ ~

Design & Typesetting by Mrs. Dawn Rouncville
Logo Creation & Design by Mrs. Doris Rome

JUST MARRIED

CD15P.

Marriages may be
made in heaven,
but the
maintenance
work is done
on earth.

♥ *Introduction* ♥

Many newlyweds believe that the intense rush of romance that they feel during their courtship and wedding days will last forever. Often they feel let down as both of them settle into the regular routine of day-to-day living and the sparking flames of romance diminish to a faint flicker...

These romantic feelings **can** be kept alive and even enhanced if one **chooses** to give one's partner time, attention, tender loving words and little gifts on a regular basis. One must remember that romance is an attitude that can be created **anytime**, **anywhere**! It does, however, require some energy and a concerted effort!

♥ *Love at first sight is nothing special.*
It's when two people have been looking at each other for
years that it becomes a miracle. ♥
*~~~ **Sam Levinson** ~~~*

If you think you have to be at some lush beach on an exotic island to feel romantic, think again. You may be missing some of the greatest opportunities for enhancing your love relationship **right at home**!

A romantic, thoughtful word or action can serve as a catalyst and immediately your relationship will be **enhanced** and **enriched**.

The secret is to ***pro-actively plan*** these expressions and to make them a habit!

This treasury of ideas will help you do just that!

♥ Yes! You can be a great, romantic lover!
♥ Yes! You can be pro-active and initiate romantic/sexual activities with your mate!
♥ Yes! You can be your spouse's greatest cheerleader and supporter!

Read on ...... Find out how!   *Ruth*

♥ *Think About Your Unique Mate* ♥

Depending on your personality and depending on your mate's, some of these ideas you will like immediately and want to use; others will not suit. **Be selective** and choose ones that you **both** will enjoy. Perhaps you should consider leaving your comfort zone in order to try new, more exotic expressions of your love.

When I first started to put these ideas into practice, I thought that my 6'3" husband would find this "corny" or perhaps "silly". I was definitely wrong! He says he is delighted with ALL my small, large and creative expressions of affirmation.

♥ *The person who sows seeds of kindness enjoys a perpetual harvest.* ♥

♥ Be Consistent in Your Love Expressions ♥

Decide how often you are going to use one of these ideas – once a month, every two weeks, once a week. If you have never done this sort of thing before, then start **slowly** and share your expressions infrequently.

♥ *Love is a decision.* ♥

You also don't want to give your mate a heart attack with all this attention!! Whatever you decide, be **consistent**! Doing **little** things more regularly is the best plan!

♥ *Little things are the hinges* ♥
on which great things happen.

♥ Save Your Best Love Expressions for Non-traditional Days ♥

Most people buy their spouses cards, gifts, etc. for Valentine's Day, Christmas, anniversaries and birthdays. Don't ignore these days, but express your most special affirmations on **ordinary** days of the year.

♥ *Marriage is an investment that pays dividends, if you pay interest.* ♥

Your spouse may assume you buy these presents on the traditional days simply because it is expected or it is your duty. Why not make your spouse feel special 365 days a year?

♥ *There's romance enough at home*
without going half a mile for it;
only people never think of it. ♥
*~~~ **Charles Dickins** ~~~*

♥ *Plan Ahead –*
Do Your Shopping All at Once ♥

Make a list of things you intend to do, note them on your personal calendar and then go shopping for all the items you need, picking them up **in one shopping trip**. Doing this will save you time and energy.

Collect items that you will use over the next two to three months and keep them in a special secret place. Planning ahead will keep you **focused**, **organized** and **consistent** in your expressions.

♥ *You will never find time for anything.*
If you want time, you must make it. ♥
~~~ ***Charles Burton***~~~

♥ Use a Calender ♥

Keep a personal calendar on which you keep track of what affirmation/gift you gave your mate each week or month. This will ensure that you do not duplicate the same idea too soon and will also help to keep yourself accountable.

♥ Plan to succeed - or plan to fail. ♥

♥ Budget Money for These Love Gifts ♥

You will note that many of the ideas in this book require very little money (most ideas cost under $5.00). These expressions do not have to be expensive or involve elaborate events - remember it is the thought that counts! Don't assume that the bigger the gift is, the more it will be appreciated. **Little** things make a **big** difference!

Remembering this will eliminate a lot of the effort and pressure out of sharing these expressions. Be assured, each time you creatively affirm your mate inside or outside of the bedroom, you are making a deposit in your relationship or "love bank" as some have called it.

Don't use the excuse that you can't afford these little gifts. Take an amount out of each paycheque and designate it as "fun" money.

Remember - what greater investment could you make than in your relationship with your spouse?

♥ *A wise lover values not so much*
the gift of the lover as
the love of the giver. ♥
~~~ **Thomas À Kempis** ~~~

♥ *Use the Element of Surprise* ♥

U se the element of surprise – Rarely, if ever, give your mate a gift directly. Surprise your partner and leave items in places that your spouse will find while alone in a private moment. Suggested places may be: on a desk, on a chair at work, on a car seat, in a daytimer, on a pillow, in a briefcase, in a gym bag, in a coat pocket, in a shoe, in a purse, etc. Your spouse will love these surprises!

♥ *Use Variety* ♥

U se variety. If you use a candy and a card one week, don't use that idea again for many weeks. Keeping track on your calendar will remind you of what you did when. Any great idea overused, soon becomes boring!

♥ Kind words can be short and easy to speak
but their echoes are truly endless. ♥
*~~~ **Mother Theresa** ~~~*

♥ When Appropriate Involve Your Children ♥

From time to time, when appropriate, let your children in on your plans for affirmation. Let them go shopping with you, or help you make a card. By involving your children, you will model ideas and skills they can use in the future with their own mates.

♥ *The most valuable gift you can give another is example.* ♥

By sharing your own **enthusiasm** toward romantic things, you will communicate the wholesomeness of marital love and that it is not something that is dirty or boring.

(Maybe you should consider asking yourself what kind of messages you are presently giving your children about love, sex and romance.)

♥ *Have Fun!* ♥

Most of all, keep in mind that this should be **fun**! Make these little expressions humorous at times. **Relax** – remember your mate is your best friend. These expressions of love are meant for a target audience of one - your own spouse - in your own private moments.

(P.S. - Note: Some of the following ideas are followed by a ... That means **YOU** fill in the blank, use your imagination ... **Oh la la!**)

Marriage is an empty box. It remains empty unless you put more in than you take out.

♥ Idea 1 ♥

Make a tape of your mate's favorite love song or a song that is meaningful to both of you. Put it in your spouse's tape deck in the car. Turn the player on so when your beloved starts the ignition, your special song will be heard first thing in the morning. What a great way to start their day!

Also develop a collection of "mood" music for use in your bedroom – keep these tapes under the bed for easy access. Make up one tape of all your favorite songs.

♥ *Marriage is like a violin.*
After the beautiful music is over,
the strings are still attached. ♥

♥ *Idea 2* ♥

Put a man's tie around the steering wheel of his car with this note attached:

"If love is the tie that binds, then I'm **BOUND!**"

♥ *Idea 3* ♥

Attach several balloons to the bottom of the garage door - each with a meter of string and an appropriate written message. They will magically rise in the air when the garage door is opened. **"Welcome Home!"** they might say (a nice gesture if your mate has been away for a few days).

♥ *Love is giving someone your undivided attention.* ♥

You could also buy a helium balloon with an appropriate loving message and leave it in a place easily found (in the office, work bench, bathroom). A balloon bouquet sent to the office may also be appreciated.

♥ *Let a wife make her husband glad to come home, and let him make her sorry to see him leave.* ♥
~~~ Martin Luther ~~~

♥ *Idea 4* ♥

Frame a picture of you and your mate with the caption: "**Picture This – You and I Forever**!" (For ladies - have a glamour photo  of yourself taken, complete with fancy clothes/feathers. You'll find these packages offered at shopping malls.)

♥ *Respect is what we owe,*
love is what we give. ♥

♥ Idea 5 ♥

Does your mate enjoy sports? Can't afford the price of tickets for a live game plus babysitting costs? Then plan your own special event in the comfort of your own living room.

♥ *Let your mate know you're on their team!* ♥

Prepare an invitation for your mate. For example:

You are invited to the

Super Bowl Game

When: This Sunday – 1:00 pm.
Where: Our Living Room
Great Refreshments! Great Company!

& Outstanding Half-Time Entertainment!

♥ *Idea 6* ♥

Buy your husband a gift of fancy underwear. Attach a note: "You like me to dress nicely for bed – now it is **your** turn!" (Check out the men's brief department at Wal-Mart™. They have some great glow-in-the-dark, metallic ones for $4.95!)

♥ Idea 7 ♥

Collect candles of all shapes and sizes from garage sales and/or a dollar store. Light them **all** in your bedroom and watch the glow in your mate's eyes when walks into your room.

(One word to the wise – put a plate under each candle. You will get busy doing other things and you will find that you will be scraping up candle wax the next morning from all over your dresser or carpet ... grrr ...)

♥ *Idea 8* ♥

Plan to have a romantic breakfast in bed or meal in bed. Be an **appealing** waitress/waiter. Give exceptional service ... Wear only an attractive apron ...

Some food ideas - put Hershey Kisses™ in their cereal or take a slice of bread and use a heart-shaped cookie cutter to take the centre out of the bread. Lightly toast both sides of bread. Scramble an egg and just when the egg becomes a non-runny form, put the toast in the skillet and place the egg in the open heart of the bread to finish cooking. Another idea – use chocolate syrup/icing to write a loving message around the edge of a plate.

♥ *The greatest of these is love.* ♥
~~~ **I Cor. 13:13** ~~~

♥ Idea 9 ♥

Write your mate a **love letter** entitled, "Why I'm Glad I Married YOU!" You may wish to write these expressions in the form of a scroll or take the time to write them on the squares of the toilet paper in the bathroom. (I'm sure these words written there will attract attention and provide interesting reading.)

♥ *Idea 10* ♥

Wrap up a pair of large oven mitts and attach a note: **"Beware!** You should prepare to wear these tonight – Your mate may be too hot to handle ..." This is sure to bring a chuckle and a smile! (Or, wrap up some hot peppers, attaching a note: "You're hot stuff, too!")

♥ Idea 11 ♥

Put a hot water bottle in your mate's suitcase before leaving on a trip. Attach a note stating:

> "This is what I have to cuddle
> when you are away..... YUK!
> Hurry Home!
> I Miss You!

♥ *Life minus love equals zero.* ♥

♥ *Idea 12* ♥

L eave many packages of matches in one of your mate's coat pockets and attach a note: "What A **Match** We Are!"

♥ *Idea 13* ♥

I f your mate is a golfer, tie little candies or chocolates to each of their golf clubs (hide them under the club covers). Leave one candy on the car seat, attaching a note:

"The best **treat** is yet to come ...
hurry home!"

♥ Idea 14 ♥

Buy some massage oil and massage your stressed-out mate. Better yet, take a course together in the art of massage or purchase a book on the subject. Consider purchasing a hand-held massage machine.

♥ *Idea 15* ♥

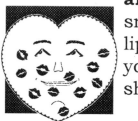 Leave sticky notes on your mate's rearview mirror, dashboard, daytimer, bathroom mirror, etc., giving them loving **messages of affirmation**. Write messages in the snow or on the car windshield. Use lipstick or wash-off markers to write your affirmations on the steamy shower door or bathroom mirror .

♥ *Idea 16* ♥

I f your mate is going away on a business trip, ask if it would be appropriate if you went along. Pay your own meals/expenses, and enjoy some time away with your spouse. Checking into how much extra it would cost to have a jacuzzi in your room might be a nice idea. Pay the difference in the room rate.

♥ *No gift is a substitute for yourself.* ♥

♥ *Idea 17* ♥

Leave loving messages on your spouse's answering machine or voice mail. Share a singing telegram. For example, use Stevie Wonder's song, "I Just Called to Say I Love You!" and hang up.

Or...

E-mail your mate at work.

(P.S. Make sure your message goes to your mate only. One lady shared that her loving message reached the computer of every member in the office - needless to say, there was much teasing!)

♥ Idea 18 ♥

I f your mate goes on business trips or away to a conference or retreat, pack little surprise gifts in his/her suitcase. Put little notes on each gift revealing on which day they are to open them.

Some ideas for little gifts:

♥ A tube of Close-Up™ toothpaste.
♥ A bar of Caress™ soap.
♥ Pin loving notes on their underwear.
♥ A bag of Hershey Kisses™.

> ♥ *Love does not die easily. It is a living thing.*
> *It thrives in the face of life's hazards,*
> *save one thing, neglect.* ♥
> ~~~ **James D. Bryden** ~~~

♥ Idea 19 ♥

Buy your mate a crocheted snowflake decoration or purchase anything with a snowflake motif. Write a note telling why your beloved is God's unique creation and His gift to you.

♥ Idea 20 ♥

Change the light bulbs in your bedroom. Purchase black light bulbs – everything white in your bedroom will glow in the dark. It creates a nice ambience. At Christmas, change your light bulbs to red and green – "Tis the season to celebrate!"

♥ Idea 21 ♥

Wrap up your mate's favorite tea bags in an attractive mug and tell them you'll meet them in a nearby teahouse at a mutually convenient time. Or make them a book of $5.00 coupon/gift certificates from various local restaurants. Tell them you want to enjoy a milkshake, coffee or soda at each one at a mutually convenient time.

♥ *Idea 22* ♥

Buy a Time-Out™ chocolate bar and write a note of appreciation saying, "Just taking **"Time-Out"** to tell you how much I appreciate ......" (Affirm a positive character quality or a recent thoughtful action.)

♥ Idea 23 ♥

Buy books on romance/sex and read them together. If you don't like to do so together, read them separately and then come together to discuss. Start small if you are not avid readers – try reading a chapter a week. Leave the book by a favorite chair or in the bathroom. Tie a bottle of spice to the books - with the note: "Just want to spice up our relationship a bit ... let's read together."

Some suggestions include:

Men and Sex (Clifford and Joyce Penner)
Mars & Venus in the Bedroom (John Gray)
The Five Love Languages (Gary Chapman)

Or start a tradition of buying each other a significant, special book every anniversary. Inscribe a special message in it noting why you bought this book and why you thought they would enjoy it.

♥ *Idea 24* ♥

Buy some Excel™ gum. Write a note: "Just wanted to tell you, you **"EXCEL"** at ... and I love you for it!"

♥ *If you would be loved, love and be loveable.* ♥
~~~ ***Benjamin Franklin*** ~~~

♥ *Idea 25* ♥

K eep a calendar of your special times together throughout the year. Give this calendar to your mate with pictures/notations about the special time/moments you have spent together and spend some time reminiscing together.

♥ *Seize the moment -*
Hone your romantic spirit. ♥

Look for more elaborate or special calendars on for half-price after Christmas. Save your yearly calendars and review past events for years to come.

> ♥ *Love can perish ...*
> *when there is no time for romantic activity ...*
> *when a man and his wife forget*
> *how to talk to each other.* ♥
> ~~~ **James Dobson** ~~~

♥ Idea 26 ♥

Buy a SKOR™ chocolate bar and attach a note: "WOW! You **"Skor"** big with me! Thanks for spending quality time with me." (Or whatever you wish to express appreciation for...)

♥ *Encouragement is oxygen to the soul.* ♥

♥ *Idea 27* ♥

Write poems to your lover to express your feelings. If you aren't a poet yourself, find good poetry books and read them to your mate in person or on tape.

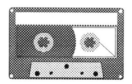

♥ Idea 28 ♥

Spray your mate's favorite perfume/aftershave on their pillow before you leave for an overnighter or retreat. Also hide a card under the pillowcase. They'll be sure to find it as soon as they put their head down ... and have sweet dreams!

♥ Idea 29 ♥

Spell the words "I Love You" with candies on your mate's favorite chair, office desk or car seat. (Use Smarties™, Hershey Kisses™, cinnamon hearts, etc.)

> ♥ *Love every day.*
> *Each one is so short*
> *and they are so few.* ♥
> ~~~ **Norman Vincent Peale** ~~~

♥ *Idea 30* ♥

Find two mismatched socks and wrap them up with the following note:

"Two socks seldom match for life ...
sure glad we are!"

Purchase a brand new pair of matched socks for your spouse and include them with this gift.

♥ Idea 31 ♥

Wrap up a firelog and leave it on your mate's car seat with the attached note:

"Meet you at the fireplace at 8:30."
or
"Come on, Baby! - Light My Fire!"

B uy your spouse tulips or tulip bulbs. Attach a note: "To the tu-lips I love – From the tu-lips you love."

Or purchase a plant not huge and flourishing. Attach this note: "Although, like this plant, our relationship may not be perfect and sometimes we feel a little wilted, I would like our relationship to thrive with some love and care. Plants, like people, need a lot of love and affection – so let this be a symbol of our love – and let's keep growing together."

♥ *Keep your eyes wide open before marriage and half shut afterwards.* ♥

♥ *Idea 33* ♥

W rap up a body sponge with an attached note:

"Would love to **shower** my love on you tonight."

♥ *Idea 34* ♥

Plan **"theme nights."** Possible themes: Western Night, Hockey Night, or Eskimo Night. Plan your food and decorate your bedroom using the theme idea. With simple, yet appropriate decorations, props and clothing, you can turn an ordinary night into a real celebration. Keep your partner guessing what your bedroom will look like next. Have great fun in the confines of your own home!

♥ Idea 35 ♥

Purchase liquid body soap (Avon™ sells this.) It is in a roll-on container in various colors – Have fun "painting" each other in the shower. You may find you will discover some artistic ability you didn't know you had! Also, check out chocolate body paints at lingerie stores.

♥ *Love is like a smile -*
neither have any value - until given away. ♥

♥ Idea 36 ♥

Plan an Oscar night. Make a little Oscar out of foil and present your mate with a note:

"And the Award for the Best Loving, Caring Husband/Wife is _____."

Perhaps do this event when the Oscars are on television. Make it a yearly event.

♥ *Idea 37* ♥

Purchase a bottle of natural spring water. Put a few drops of red food coloring in it and wrap the bottle with fancy cellophane or tissue paper. Attached the following note:

"Drink this "Love Potion" and instantly become a churning passionate lover. This high-potency "Romance Enhancer" will enliven your love hormones and will unleash the powers of love."

"Caution: Use sparingly or you'll need a fire extinguisher to douse the flames of desire."

♥ *Success in marriage*
consists not only in
finding the right person -
but also in being the right person. ♥

♥ *Idea 38* ♥

Put a small bottle of Aspirin™ in a place your mate will find it. Attach a note:

"I took care of my headache ...
Looking forward to tonight ..."

♥ *Idea 39* ♥

Put a fishing tackle box and other fishing equipment in a conspicuous place for your mate to discover. Attach a loving note stating:

"You are a perfect catch!"

♥ *Idea 40* ♥

Have a **fashion show**. Model for your husband all of the different pieces of lingerie you have collected over the years. You will be sure to have a captive audience! Either one of you can provide the commentary.

♥ *The best gifts are always*
tied with heartstrings. ♥

♥ Idea 41 ♥

Plant a tree on a special occasion, anniversary, or when you buy your first home. Give your tree a name and it will remind you of your growing love. Or plant a rose bush on every anniversary.

♥ *Love is the fairest bloom
   in God's garden.* ♥

♥ Idea 42 ♥

Buy your spouse several apples or put one in your mate's coat pocket. Attach a message taped to a toothpick and stick it into the apple: "What an **apple**-ing sex partner you are" or "You are the apple of my eye."

♥ *Kind words never wear out the tongue.* ♥

♥ Idea 43 ♥

Buy several packages of Lifesavers™ and place them all around the house for your mate to find throughout the day. Attach an appropriate love note: "You're a real lifesaver ... I would be alone and lonely without you." Or "You're a real lifesaver because you ..." (Identify a positive quality or a thoughtful action done by your partner.)

♥ Idea 44 ♥

Plan a mystery night or **"Date with Mate"** night. Write this in their daytimer, giving them lots of notice. Give them clues about the event and make sure you tell them what time/what type of clothes to wear (formal/casual/sporty, etc). Make all the arrangements / reservations / baby-sitters, etc. They will love the suspense!

♥ *Love is an action, an activity. It is not a feeling.* ♥
~~~ **M. Scott Peck** ~~~

♥ *Idea 45* ♥

Make reservations at a hotel during the **day**. You can often get a special day rate (you don't stay overnight). Plan an exciting afternoon without kids and without having to pay a babysitter (if the children are in school). Go for a swim, relax in the jacuzzi, go out for lunch and ...

♥ *Our greatest danger in life is in permitting the urgent things to crowd out the important.* ♥
~~~ ***C. Hummel*** ~~~

♥ *Idea 46* ♥

Give your mate a new pair of gloves/mittens and attach a note saying: "I want to hold your hand ..." or "We're a perfect pair."

♥ *No act of kindness,
no matter how small, is ever wasted.* ♥
~~~ ***Aesop*** ~~~

♥ *Idea 47* ♥

Purchase a box of chocolate Ovation™ after-dinner mints. Attach a card: "I'd like to give you a standing ovation because ......"

♥ *Kindness is the oil*
that takes the friction out of life. ♥

♥ *Idea 48* ♥

P ut an outdoor firepit in your back yard. You and your mate can have many a romantic late night without needing a babysitter.

♥ *To keep the fire burning brightly, keep the two logs together,*
Near enough to keep each other warm,
And far enough apart - about a finger's breath -
For breathing room.
Good fire, good marriage ... same rule. ♥
*~~~ **Marnie Reed Crowell** ~~~*

♥ *Idea 49* ♥

Perhaps for some reason(s) you have been very busy and have neglected your special quality time with your mate. Purchase some shoestring licorice and tie the pieces together to form long strings. Then tie many knots in them. Attach a note:

"Sorry, I've been so tied up lately ...
Let's plan some special time together this week!"

♥ *Idea 50* ♥

Purchase a box of Thrills™ gum and attach a note: "I still love the **thrills and chills** when I make love to you!"

♥ *A psychologist says*
kissing is where two people get so close together
they can't see anything wrong with each other. ♥

♥ Idea 51 ♥

Make a homemade card and tape pennies on the entire interior surface of the card. Write the following message within:

"If I had a penny for every thoughtful action and word you have given me ...
I'd be a millionaire!
Thanks for your constant affirmation!"

♥ Idea 52 ♥

Create a homemade certificate on your computer. For example:

Institute of Love and Romance proudly names:

_____

As **THE WORLD'S GREATEST LOVER**
for making the earth shake,
the sky explode and the heavens tremble.
No one does it better!

Or
SWEETHEART OF THE YEAR AWARD
Presented to:

___

For recognizing my needs and desires,
For bringing out the best in me,
For your consistent love and attention,
For your ongoing care and concern.
Therefore, be it resolved that, in my eyes and
heart, you are declared the most worthy title of
SWEETHEART OF THE YEAR!

♥ Idea 53 ♥

Purchase satin sheets or silk pillowcases. They provide a nice special feeling in bed. Watch for them when they go on sale after Christmas.

♥ Idea 54 ♥

Make up a **coupon book** of practical acts of kindness that you will do for your mate. Volunteer to do the jobs they dislike doing the most! Or make up a list of chores on small pieces of paper. Let them pick from the jar each day for a week and tell them you will cheerfully do that chore for them that day.

♥ *Kindness is like snow -*
it beautifies everything it covers. ♥

♥ *Idea 55* ♥

H ave a **treasure hunt**. Ask your mate to go around the house to find clues about your special surprise. If you are planning to go away for a private getaway, cut up pieces of a map and have them find all the pieces and then guess where you are taking them. Hide Sweet Escape™ chocolate bars around the house and attach a note stating: "I'm looking forward to our Sweet Escape together."

♥ Idea 56 ♥

Tape a loving message over the switch plate in your bedroom or in their bathroom: "You light up my life" or "You Flick My Switch!"

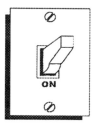

♥ *Idea 57* ♥

Put the following note on your mate's computer: "I have a power surge whenever I'm with you!"

Purchase a mouse pad with a loving message inscribed on it, or have one made with your picture on it.

♥ Idea 58 ♥

Plan a **midnight picnic** inside or outside your home. Choose an unusual location: in your car, trailer, or in front of the fireplace. If you  choose to go outside, put a blanket on the ground and put lighted red tea candles around you both in the shape of a heart. Enjoy!

♥ *Idea 59* ♥

Mail your spouse a card at work filled with confetti. Attach a note: **"Let's Celebrate** … Our Anniversary" or some other special occasion. Wrap up some streamers and a party hat as well.

♥ *A smile adds face value.* ♥

♥ *Idea 60* ♥

Buy your mate a new wristwatch. Engrave the back of the watch with the words:

"I'll always have **time** for you!"

♥ *Life is not a rehearsal -
Do it right the first time.* ♥

♥ *Idea 61* ♥

Put a dollar in a decorated jar on your dresser or night table every time you make love – what a collection you will have at the end of the year. Buy something special for both of you to celebrate or save money toward an exotic trip.

♥ *Kindness is one thing you can't give away -*
It always comes back. ♥

♥ Idea 62 ♥

Wrap up some batteries and attach a note: "Time to re-charge our relationship. Let's plan a getaway soon."

♥ *Idea 63* ♥

Buy him a new tape measure and attach a note: "This tape measure isn't long enough to measure my love for you."

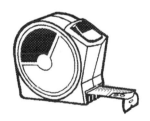

♥ *Idea 64* ♥

Purchase a bottle of Eno™ or a bottle of Tums™. Attach a note:

"My heart "burns" for you!"

♥ Idea 65 ♥

At Easter purchase plastic Easter eggs and write little notes inside them telling your mate why he/she is an **Egg**-ceptional Mate, Parent and Lover. Hide them around the house and have your spouse search for them.

♥ *Idea 66* ♥

Create a custom parking ticket. Place it on your mate's windshield. At first this might be upsetting, but the message on the other side says, "Let's go parking ...... at 9:30 p.m."

♥ *Idea 67* ♥

Renew your wedding vows at a public or private ceremony. Plan the occasion in an unusual venue: in a romantic log chapel, on a beach, or at a botanical garden.

♥ *Idea 68* ♥

G o out for a progressive dinner - go to one restaurant for appetizers, another for the main meal, another for dessert.

♥ *Idea 69* ♥

Plan a honeymoon evening. Decorate your bedroom with posters or decorations from where you spent your honeymoon. Relive the beautiful memories. Watch your wedding video and look through your wedding photos.

♥ *The heart that loves
is always young.* ♥

♥ *Idea 70* ♥

Purchase matching clothes of some kind (hats, jackets, sweatshirts). You'll receive many compliments! Having matching hats, towels, or pillowcases monogrammed is also a nice gesture.

♥ Idea 71 ♥

Cut up little pieces of red or yellow yarn and leave them on a trail throughout your house. Attach a note to the first one: "Follow this string and you will find a beautiful thing!" You decide what the surprise will be. Or use rose petals or foot prints to make a trail.

♥ Love may not make the world go round but it sure makes the trip worthwhile. ♥

♥ *Idea 72* ♥

Plan an old-fashioned date. Go horseback riding or on a sleigh ride. Watch an old-fashioned movie. Visit a museum. Bake something from scratch.

♥ *True love is always costly.* ♥

♥ Idea 73 ♥

Have a **"Fit for a King/Queen Day."** Treat your mate like royalty. Buy him/her a Royale™ chocolate bar. Tell them, "Your wish is my command for the day." Wait on them hand and foot. Serve them chocolates, fruit, etc. on a silver platter. Make them a crown, just for fun!

♥ Idea 74 ♥

Take a course together. Look in adult education brochures and take a course that explores a new interest for both of you. Wrap up a gift certificate for your mate. Sign up for a Marriage Encounter™ or marriage enrichment weekend.

♥ *You can give without loving,*
but you cannot love without giving. ♥
~~~ **Amy Carmichael** ~~~

♥ *Idea 75* ♥

Make an invitation for your mate to "**Fantasy Island**." Plan an event/ evening where you make some of your spouse's sexual fantasies come true. Decorate your room in an island theme - Buy a tape of ocean waves for background music. Wear an eye-catching bathing suit. Spread out a beach towel, umbrella, beach ball, etc.

♥ Idea 76 ♥

Buy your mate a dictionary. Go through and highlight all the loving words or words to describe them. Put a note on the front cover telling what page to turn to and then at each page give them direction as to what page to go to next.

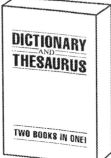

♥ *Idea 77* ♥

U sing the letters of your spouse's name, write an acronym describing your mate and their wonderful qualities.

For example: SIMON -
S - sensational sensual lover
I - irresistible irreplaceable husband
M - ......

♥ *Idea 78* ♥

Spend some time laughing together. Purchase John McPherson's cartoon book entitled *McPherson's Marriage Album* (Zondervan Publishing) and cuddle up in bed and read it together.

♥ *If you laugh a lot, when you get older your wrinkles will be in the right places.* ♥

♥ Idea 79 ♥

Buy your partner a bag of gourmet popcorn and attach a note:

"Loving Thoughts Of You Keep Popping
Into My Mind All Day Long!
Hurry Home!"

♥ *Kind words fall lightly -*
but have great weight. ♥

♥ *Idea 80* ♥

Take a mini-vacation together (on video). Go to your local library or travel agent and ask for promotional videos about a place you and your mate have always dreamed of going. Watch the video together, then talk about how you are going to budget/plan for this exciting adventure together.

♥ *Unshared joy is an unlighted candle.* ♥

Obtain some pamphlets and posters of your romantic destination and hang them up in your room or on the fridge.

♥ Idea 81 ♥

Name a star after your spouse. Check with a local or regional Space Sciences Centre or observatory for more information on how to do this. Every time you take those romantic midnight strolls, you can point out your star to your mate. Or cut out and hang little stars from the ceiling of your bedroom. Write on each star a reason why your mate is the "Star of Your Show."

♥ Idea 82 ♥

Purchase some firecrackers or birthday sparklers. Wrap them up for your mate and attach a note: "When I make love to you, the fireworks explode." ... or whatever other appropriate message you choose. Take these firecrackers to a secluded area and light them. Then ... create some sparks of your own!

♥ *Idea 83* ♥

Give your mate a card stating, "It's Time for a Check-up." Tell them that **you** are their doctor and it is time for you to "check" them out. Wrap up a box with a magnifying glass, some pill bottles filled with heart candies, some bandages to kiss their hurts all better and some great-smelling lotion to massage them with, and ...

Or - come down with a severe case of Spring Fever.
Tell them the only cure for this illness is to stay in
bed all day with **YOU!**

♥ *Idea 84* ♥

Purchase 11 red roses and one white one or purchase eleven blue pens and one red one. Attach a note: "You always stand out in a crowd."

♥ *I can live two months on a good compliment.* ♥
~~~ **Mark Twain** ~~~

♥ *Idea 85* ♥

Give a sweet gift to your HONEY. Wrap up a jar of honey and make a card using HoneyComb™ cereal to form letters. Tell your mate their affirmations are as "sweet as honey."

♥ Idea 86 ♥

Wrap up John Gray's book: *Men are from Mars, Women are from Venus* and attach a Mars™ candy bar with a note stating that you would like to learn more about life on each other's planet.

♥ *Idea 87* ♥

Make a peanut butter and jelly sandwich and put in your mate's lunch kit. Attach the note:

"You're sweet as jelly and I'm stuck on you!"

♥ *God is the only third party*
that can make a marriage work. ♥

♥ *Idea 88* ♥

Wrap up a PEP™ bar and attach a note: "WOW!!! You sure had a lot of pep last night - Sure enjoyed your passionate lovemaking!"

♥ *Laughter is the shock absorber*
that eases the blows of life. ♥

♥ *Idea 89* ♥

Purchase a Gold Mine™ chocolate bar or purchase some special commemorative coins for your mate. Attach a note:

"I sure hit a gold mine when I met you!"

♥ *Idea 90* ♥

Take a cruise (yes, the Caribbean would be nice, but if you can't work that into your budget, take a harbor cruise or a cruise on a lake). Go canoeing or rafting. Send your mate an invitation: "I'd like to go CRUISING with you..." and then give the details.

♥ *Idea 91* ♥

Take a moment to help your husband understand you and your sexual needs better. Wrap up a birthday sparkler and a candle. Attach a note asking him to light both at the same time. Tell him the sparkler represents him and the candle represents you in bed. This object lesson may provide a good word picture for your husband and may stimulate some interesting discussion.

♥ *Idea 92* ♥

Purchase some sunflowers for your spouse. Attach a note:

"You're the sunshine of my life...
and
P.S. - You have a
cute little moon, too."

♥ *Idea 93* ♥

Had a few disagreements? Some heated discussions? Wrap up a bag of Werthers™ butterscotch candies. Attach a note:

"Werther we agree or disagree....I'm still in love with you and I am committed to you."

♥ *Marriages may be made in heaven -*
but so are thunder and lightning! ♥

♥ *Idea 94* ♥

Put a bulletin board on the back of your bedroom door or inside your private medicine cabinet door. Write personal love messages on it. Both partners can participate. For example, Mary's Massage Parlour will be open from 9:30 to 10:30 tonight. Would love to SEE you!

♥ *Love is the only "game"*
two can play and win. ♥

One couple who used this idea had had a very busy schedule and the wife wrote, "Mary's Massage Parlour has been forced to close due to lack of clientele ..."

(This idea will probably work best if your children can't read yet!)

HAPPINESS IS BEING MARRIED TO YOUR BEST FRIEND

♥ *Idea 95* ♥

Plan to spend an exciting night at the raceway or stock car races. Give your mate a card: "My engine still revs for you and my heart races when I'm with you. Fasten your seatbelt and get ready for an exhilarating evening with me!"

♥ *Idea 96* ♥

Wrap up a jar of your partner's favorite jam. Attach a note: "When I'm in a jam, I know I can always count on you!"

♥ *"Two are better than one because they have a good return for their work. If one falls down, his friend can help him up."* ♥
~~~ ***Ecclesiastes 4:9-10 (NIV)*** ~~~

♥ *Idea 97* ♥

Don't feel like eating at home? Make your spouse an invitation stating:

"I've made my favorite thing for supper - a reservation!"

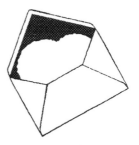

♥ *Idea 98* ♥

Go on a Million Dollar Date. Pretend your rich uncle has just died and left you both one million dollars. Spend an evening pretending you are a millionaire. Test drive the car of your dreams, go through expensive show homes, go to an expensive restaurant for dessert and coffee and then go home and talk about how these things wouldn't make you happy - but how a strong, loving relationship would.

Give your spouse a million-dollar hug and kiss and...

♥ *The art of love is largely the art of persistence.* ♥
~~~ **Dr. Albert Ellis** ~~~

♥ Idea 99 ♥

Do a survey. Wrap up three or four different pairs of attractive and alluring ladies' panties. Leave these on your husband's car seat or on his pillow with the following card:

"Hello, Mr. _____. I am doing a survey. Could you spare a few minutes of your time? Your opinion is very important to me."

"Could you please give your comments on what you like about these garments and which garment would be your favorite." Undoubtedly, you will get some interesting feedback.

♥ *A successful marriage requires*
falling in love many times
always with the same person. ♥
~~~ **Mignon McLaughlin** ~~~

♥ *Idea 100* ♥

Purchase a new hand-held calculator for your mate and leave it on their desk. Attach the following note: "Any way I calculate it, you're the world's greatest lover!"

♥ *How do I love thee?*
Let me count the ways. ♥
~~~ *E. Barrett Browning* ~~~

♥ *Idea 101* ♥

Cut out a large set of red lips from construction paper and put in an appropriate place for your mate to find. Attach a note: "If your lips aren't busy tonight ... why not bring them on over to my face?"

♥ *Kiss - a contraction of the mouth due to an enlargement of the heart.* ♥

Appendix

♥ *Know someone getting married soon?*

♥ *Going to a bridal shower?*

This book makes a very practical, thoughtful gift to help the new bride or groom begin and maintain a healthy, growing romantic life.

Look no further ......

Buy this book as a shower gift. Read some of the ideas at the shower - this is sure to get some chuckles. (Order form at back of book.)

♥ Great anniversary gift!

♥ Great stocking stuffer!

♥ Great little gift for your daughters or granddaughters!

Order Information

- ♥ Fax orders: (780) 987-4786

- ♥ Telephone orders: (780) 987-4786

- ♥ On-line orders: clardfec@netcom.ca

- ♥ Postal orders: Two-gether™
                         Box 5422
                         Devon, Alberta
                         Canada T9G 1Y1

Special Note:
Want to share a creative idea for romance?
Send it to the above address ... I'd love to hear from you!

Name: _____

Address: _____

City: _____ Prov:_____ Postal Code _____

Telephone: (   ) _____

(   ) copy (ies) of Romance 101 @ $9.99 $_____

Shipping $2.50 for 1-3 copies $_____
Add $2.50 for each additional copy
Total $_____
Orders Must Be Prepaid

❑ Visa   ❑ Cheque (Cheques payable to Two-gether™ Publishing)

| | | | | | | | | | | | | | | | | | | | | | | |

Visa Card Number   Expiry   **VISA**

Cardholder Signature _____

Ruth Clarence
presents one-day seminars entitled:

Two-gether Intimately...
Understanding & Meeting Your
Husband's Sexual Needs

If you are interested in finding out how this seminar
could be presented in your area, please contact:

Two-gether™
780-987-4786 (phone or fax)

Two-gether
Publishing

Another book by Ruth Clarence

Two-gether Intimately...
Understanding & Meeting
Your Husband's Sexual Needs

Check website for order details: www.two-gether.com

Two-gether Publishing has made every effort to trace ownership of all quotes/ideas.
In the event of a question arising from the use of a quote,
we regret any error made and will be pleased to make the
necessary correction in future editions of the book.
Back photo by Glamor Magic.